GOERS' GUIDE

TO PARLIAMENTARY PROCEDURE

BY SUE GOERS

Professional Registered Parliamentarian

Goers' Guide to Parliamentary Procedure
Copyright © 1990 by Sue Goers
Printed and bound in the United States of America. All rights reserved. No part of this book may be reproduced in any form or by any electronic or mechanical means including information storage and retrieval systems without permission in writing from the publisher, except by a reviewer, who may quote brief passages in a review. Published by Pinkerton Publishing, P.O. Box 5121, Godfrey, Illinois 62035. First edition. Third printing.
ISBN 0-9624072-0-8
Library of Congress Catalog Card Number: 89-63630

DEDICATION

This book is dedicated to my partner and best friend, my husband A.J. whose encouragement and strength throughout our lives have been a constant inspiration.

Contents

ACKNOWLEDGMENTS

I gratefully acknowledge my debt to Lars Hoffman and his wife Judy for providing just the right combination of tea and sympathy, optimistic enthusiasm and constructive criticism in all the right places. Without their encouragement I might have given up after the first draft.

I appreciate greatly the advice and support of Clare Finck, as well as her generous permission to use the treasurer's report form she developed many years ago.

Thanks are due also, to my son Matt and his friends for donating their rec. room during one whole summer so I could write in peace.

Last, but certainly not least in my heart, is my friend and teacher Ula Brazier, whose soft spoken, "It's very good, Sue," lit up my life and validated my ticket! I have learned much from this lovely lady and I acknowledge it here.

PREFACE

I was sitting in a meeting of my local club many, many Januarys ago, when another member moved to discharge the Christmas Party Committee at the conclusion of her report. She cited *Robert's Rules of Order* and waved a little paperback book to support her contention that a committee must be discharged of its duties by a formal vote of the assembly. It seemed a silly notion that we should spend any time disbanding a committee whose reason for being was finished.

A funny thing happened on the way to discovering that a special committee is automatically dissolved when it gives its final report – I fell head over heels in love with the finite intricacies of these rules and their seemingly infinite applications.

A not-so-funny thing happened, too. I searched high and low and could not find a book in simple language, in laymen's terms, about parliamentary procedure.

Year after year I hear the same question from my students and clients. "Where can we find a simple, easy-to-understand book on basic procedure?" *Goers' Guide* is such a book and it is equally suitable for the student, the club member and anyone who seeks to become acquainted with parliamentary law.

INTRODUCTION

Parliamentary law has a long and distinguished history dating back to the Fifth Century and, quite possibly, even earlier. Anglo-Saxon tribal warriors gathered together to make "bye-laws" and tend to the business at hand, namely invading Britain.

In 1066 the Normans added a more formal and structured means of government that included councils and meetings at the call of the king. Not a democracy to be sure, but things were definitely headed in the right direction. By the Thirteenth Century, a forerunner of the House of Commons was instituted and by the Fourteenth Century both Houses of Parliament, the House of Commons and the House of Lords, were firmly and permanently in place.

Today's parliamentary rules are the sum total of an interesting evolution of procedure handed down through the centuries. Some of the rules have changed drastically and some have remained almost entirely intact for hundreds of years, through hundreds of governing bodies. For instance, the notion of taking one subject at a time can be dated back to the 1500s.

A founding father and resident genius to the Continental Congress, Thomas Jefferson wrote his *Manual of Parliamentary Practice* for use in the United States Senate. *Jefferson's Manual* is generally accepted as the first American treatise on the subject.

For many years *Jefferson's Manual* was the accepted parliamentary authority not only in legislatures, but in smaller, deliberative assemblies. As the country grew so did the number of small societies. It soon became apparent that the rules for law makers were far too cumbersome for these small groups.

Cushing's Manual was intended to serve regular deliberative societies of a non-legislative nature, and it was the precursor of *Robert's Rules of Order* (written in 1876 by General Henry M. Robert). An updated version of *Robert's Rules* still forms the basis for parliamentary practice in clubs, societies, and assemblies all across this nation.

Subsequently, there have been many authors who have written on the subject and some are considered authorities, such as DeMeter, Sturgis, Strother, and Grumme. While each one has added his or her own variations and interpretations of the rules, their basic knowledge inevitably stems from Robert.

Therefore, the principles offered in *Goers' Guide* are, in general, a consensus of the major parliamentary authorities of the day. However, on those points where a difference of opinion exists among established parliamentarians, this text will invariably come down on the side of *Robert's Rules of Order Newly Revised* which is considered by this author to be the last word on parliamentary matters.

Subjects in *Goers' Guide* are arranged so that you may quickly locate areas of particular interest and find wording to help you immediately employ new information and skills.

This is by no means an exhaustive treatise on parliamentary procedure. It is intended, rather, to be a beginner's manual, easy to read and understand, and will guide the beginner through meetings. It is intended as a hands on enabler – a tool – to be used until such time as the beginner is conversant with these fundamentals and is ready to pursue more in-depth study.

A plumber fixing a leak with the wrong set of wrenches may eventually get the job done, but he is likely to have a new leak in the very near future – and all because he lacked the proper tools for the task. A banker trying to fix that leak, lacking proper tools and experience, will likely have not only a new leak but a burst pipe, or worse, and will end up hiring a plumber to fix the plumbing as well as a carpenter to replace the soggy floor boards – and all because he lacked the proper tools.

So it is with parliamentary procedure. An organization may stumble along for some time using improper or incorrect procedure with no apparent adversity. Then one day, a controversy arises and trouble bursts onto the scene, inundating the organization. As often as not, that is the situation when a professional parliamentarian is called. This text provides the proper tools to enable the layman member to jump into the fray, as it were, with assurance and confidence.

If you have just been elected secretary, for example, you will find what you need to know about writing minutes in Chapter Six. If you are serving on a committee or public board, you will want to pay special attention to Chapter Seven.

Members often indicate a suspicion about proper procedure. "We don't need that fancy parliamentary stuff. We're all friends here." Parliamentarians frequently hear similar remarks when they are called in to unravel a tangle in the friendship.

The fact is, if we want to remain friends, then we had better establish at least a modicum of decorum and order. We can be pals over dinner, but we had better be respected colleagues during business deliberations. When we show courtesy to and respect for our fellow member, we distinguish ourselves as civilized, intelligent free men and women secure in our methodology. In short – democracy works!

Democracy works best, however, when all parties understand the rules and elect to abide by them. Anything a majority wants to achieve can reasonably be accomplished through due process of the rules. There is something thrilling in the knowledge that some of the world's greatest historical figures have deliberated most of humankind's major dilemmas within the framework of these same basic rules.

Chapter 1

Principles, Decorum, and Terminology

Members of organizations of all types assemble at prescribed times and places in order to consider issues of specific and direct concern to the objectives of the organizations. There are many kinds of assemblies, but most of them fall into one of the following categories.

1. Mass Meetings, held for the purpose of accomplishing certain goals and objectives of common interest to those in attendance.

2. Legislative bodies, meeting to enact the laws of the land.

3. Meetings of an organization in convention when delegates representing various components of the organization come together.

4. Meetings of an established organization meeting at least quarterly or more often.

This book concerns itself with the last type, meetings of an organized society. Conventions deserve an entire treatise unto themselves and so will not be discussed. However, the motions found later in this book would, in the main, be applicable in the meetings of a convention.

Legislative bodies necessarily function under a more elaborate set of parliamentary rules designed to handle the immense work load characteristic of legislatures.

The average American is most likely to have some experience with meetings of an established society.

BASIC PRINCIPLES

There are some basic principles of parliamentary law which have been accepted by civilized people for many centuries. These are the underpinnings upon which orderly deliberations are built.

> ### THE FOUR BASIC PRINCIPLES OF PARLIAMENTARY PROCEDURE
>
> 1. Consider one thing at a time.
> 2. Ensure justice, courtesy, and equal treatment to all members.
> 3. Serve the will of the majority.
> 4. Preserve the right of the minority to be heard.

1. **Consider one thing at a time.** A logical and orderly process is basic to the transaction of business in any meeting. Therefore a society, according to accepted parliamentary procedure, may only consider one question at a time. Various parliamentary motions may be applied to a question during deliberations, in which case the particular motion offered becomes the immediately pending question, and, therefore, the only one to be considered at the moment.

2. **Ensure justice, courtesy, and equal treatment to all members.** All members enjoy the same basic rights and privileges of membership and have at their disposal the same procedural options and opportunities. Courteous and polite behavior, regardless of the intensity of divergent opinion, is expected at all times in any meeting. Parliamentary meetings offer ample opportunity for the effective expression of opinion.

3. **Serve the will of the majority.** Probably the most basic tenet of democracy is the concept of majority rule. In a society enjoying a free exchange of ideas, with maximum opportunity for dissenting opinion to be expressed, the will of the majority shall prevail and the minority is compelled to acquiesce.

4. **Preserve the right of the minority to be heard.** As precious as the will of the majority is to a free society, even more passionately does that society protect and defend the right of the minority to be heard. Much conflict could be avoided by adhering faithfully to this principle.

DECORUM

The terms Mr. President and Madam President are in no way to be considered sexist or demeaning terms. Quite the contrary, they are used as terms of utmost courtesy for an esteemed office. The same holds true for all other offices and titles.

Not all organizations confer the title of President on their presiding officer. The person presiding is referred to as the *chair*, and, therefore, may be addressed as Mr. Chairman or Madam Chairman. The National Association of Parliamentarians has taken a strong stand on the matter of contrived language such as the use of "Chairperson" in reference to the presiding officer. "Chairman" is a gender neutral term even though the word "man" appears in its spelling. The terms Mr. and Madam, in this case, have nothing whatever to do with an individual's marital status. Correct procedure helps us rise above the whim of individual personalities to seek a higher purpose, namely the good of the organization. The point is to emphasize courtesy and decorum which are still valued commodities of a civilized society.

Everyone who has the floor should stand before speaking, except in very small groups. The chairman should always stand to preside and anyone giving reports or debating should stand while speaking as a courtesy to the members. Quite simply, it is easier to hear someone whose voice is carrying over the heads of the audience than it is to hear someone who is speaking into the back of another member's head.

All comments, whether reports, debate, or inquiries, should begin with *"Mr. (Madam) President."* All remarks, even inquires, are made to and through the chair. If an answer or response from another member is appropriate, the *chair* will direct the response by saying, *"Would the Treasurer please give us the figures?"* or *"Ms. Smith, could you please respond to that?"*

MEETING VERSUS SESSION

In the parliamentary context, the terms *meeting* and *session* have distinct and different meanings. A *meeting* is a separate gathering of members at one time and place with no interruption except, perhaps, a brief recess. A *session* is one or more meetings using one basic agenda, such as the sessions of a convention.

TERMINOLOGY

Parliamentary procedure has a vernacular all its own and for that reason there is a glossary at the end of this text. However, there are some terms that are so basic to a parliamentary discussion that they are listed below as well as in the glossary.

Previous Notice is a parliamentary term meaning announcement that a motion will be made at the next meeting. The notice includes the specific wording of the proposal so that members are aware of it and may plan accordingly. Notice can be given orally or may be included in the call of the meeting.

The call is official notification of the time and place of the next meeting, usually mailed to members in advance of the meeting within a time frame usually prescribed in the bylaws.

Falls to the ground is a parliamentary term meaning that a particular item of business has become null and void, as if it never happened in the first place. An example would be the case of a motion that is withdrawn before the chair has stated the motion thus placing it in the hands of the assembly.

Quorum refers to the number of members a society requires to be present at a meeting in order to legally transact business. If the bylaws lack a quorum provision, the general parliamentary rule is a majority of all the membership. In the absence of a quorum, no business can legally be transacted except to fix the time to which to adjourn, adjourn, recess and/or seek to obtain a quorum by contacting absent members during a recess.

Majority (or *two-thirds*) *vote* means more than half (or two-thirds) of those present and voting, unless the bylaws state otherwise. Abstentions are not counted in determining the vote.

RIGHTS OF MEMBERS	DUTIES OF MEMBERS
To attend meetings	To attend meetings
To vote	To obey the rules
To debate	To further the goals of the organization
To make motions	
To hold office	
To nominate	

Now that we have a base of conduct and language, we can move on to the rules by which societies govern themselves.

Chapter 2

Types of Rules

In this chapter we will look at the rules necessary to the operation of an organization. In any discussion of the rules by which a society governs itself, it is important to understand how each group of rules relates to the others.

CORPORATE CHARTER

When forming an organization one must first look to the local, state, and federal laws to see if the organization's objectives are spoken to by statute. If so, an attorney should be consulted about a corporate charter.

A corporate charter is a legal document naming the organization and clearly stating its objectives. Requirements of incorporating vary from state to state.

One of the main reasons for incorporating is to protect officers of the organization from personal liability should litigation result from an action of the group.

The corporate charter is the highest ranking set of rules in an organization and any changes to it are subject to law.

BYLAWS

Next in line of priority are the bylaws, sometimes referred to as constitution and bylaws. In most organizations there is little or no reason to have a constitution as a separate entity from the bylaws. Bylaws as we know them in the late Twentieth Century are a combination of constitutional and bylaw concepts.

Bylaws set the limits within which an organization will function. They provide the official establishment of the organization in an unincorporated society, and, in an incorporated society, they conform to the corporate charter.

In either case, the bylaws are a list of rules of sufficient importance that they are protected from change by specific requirements such as previous notice to members and a larger than usual vote.

Bylaws cannot be suspended at any time, for any reason, unless the bylaws themselves contain a rule allowing their suspension under specified circumstances.

Bylaws will vary somewhat because of the size and purpose of organizations, but the basic form and order will be the same from group to group.

The following articles are basic to bylaws:

Article I.	Name of the organization
Article II.	Object or purpose of the organization
Article III.	Members
	A. Membership classifications, if any
	B. Membership qualification
	C. Dues and fees
Article IV.	Officers
	A. List of officers and duties
	B. Nomination and election procedure
Article V.	Meetings
	A. Establish regular meetings
	B. Establish annual meeting
	C. Establish special meetings
	D. Establish Quorum
*Article VI.	Executive Board
	A. Membership composition
	B. Powers
	C. Quorum
	D. Special rules of conduct, if any
**Article VII.	Committees
Article VIII.	Parliamentary Authority
Article IX.	Amendment of the Bylaws

*It is not essential to have an article establishing an Executive Board if the organization does not have a need for one.

**The same applies to an article establishing committees.

If there is such an article on committees, there are some specific points that should be included.

- Separate sections for each committee should also include the composition and duties of members.

- A separate subsection should provide for additional committees to be established as needed.

- This article may also contain a subsection establishing an ex officio status for certain officers in connection with certain committees. *Ex officio* means "by virtue of the office." Without this status expressly bestowed in the bylaws, a president, for example, cannot vote or even attend meetings of the committees without being invited by them. A subsection on ex officio status should expressly exclude such status on the Nominating Committee. An ex officio member of a committee has all of the rights and privileges of membership but none of the obligations and is not counted in the quorum.

STANDING RULES

Standing rules pertain to specific administrative details of an organization in its day-to-day operation and not to parliamentary matters or organizational matters as covered in the bylaws.

For example, the bylaws might set the regular meeting for the third Tuesday of the month and the standing rules would establish the place and time of the meetings. Whereas the third Tuesday may be carved in the stone of the bylaws, the location and time, which are apt to change frequently, may appear in the more easily amended standing rules.

Standing rules are *adopted* by majority vote and *amended* by 2/3 vote without notice or majority vote *with* notice. They can be suspended for the duration of a meeting quite simply by a majority vote.

Chapter 3

Establishing a New Organization

In the beginning there are two or more people with similar thoughts and objectives. Through discussion they come to realize that much more can be accomplished toward their common goals if they band together in an organized and unified group. There is safety in numbers precisely because a number of individuals offers more strength than one or two individuals. Whether defending a fort or fostering an ideal, a *group* is generally more effective than an individual, and an organized and focused group is more effective than a mob. In the words of General Robert, in his *Robert's Rules of Order Newly Revised*, "Where there is no law, but every man does what is right in his own eyes, there is the least of real liberty."

Thus, a new organization is on the brink of foundation. What happens next?

They begin to organize by inviting like-minded individuals to the *first organizational meeting.*

ELECTION OF TEMPORARY OFFICERS

One of the original group presides over the meeting long enough to hold nominations and an election of a chairman pro tem, who will then preside over the election of a secretary pro tem. (For exact wording on calling a meeting to order see Chapter 6.)

No other officers are elected at this time because they are not necessary to the formation of the organization. For any meeting to be official, there must be a presiding officer and a recording officer. The above step satisfies this requirement.

BACKGROUND STATEMENT

The chair, at this point, calls on someone involved in the original organizational effort to offer background material. The chair may be best qualified for the task, in which case she may speak in this capacity.

MOTION TO ORGANIZE

After remarks on the reasons and purpose of the meeting are completed, a member should move to form a permanent society. This motion requires a second and may be debated and amended. It requires a majority of those present and voting to be adopted. This motion is simply an expression of intent and does not, in and of itself, create the organization.

CREATE A COMMITTEE TO DRAFT BYLAWS

A motion is in order to appoint a committee to draft bylaws for the new organization and to consult an attorney, if necessary, concerning incorporation.

ARRANGE THE FOLLOWING MEETING

The time, date, and place of the next meeting should be set. Since the second organizational meeting is for the express purpose of considering and adopting the proposed bylaws by which the organization comes into being, ample time should be allowed for the bylaws committee to complete its task.

SECOND MEETING

The *second organizational meeting* should include:

- Reading and approval of the minutes
- Consideration and adoption of bylaws (see note)
- Election of permanent officers as prescribed in the newly adopted bylaws

- Naming of committees
- Any other business deemed necessary by the officers and members
- Adjournment

NOTE: Consideration should be seriatim, that is paragraph by paragraph.

The bylaws committee chairman, after giving a brief description of his committee deliberations, reads the proposed bylaws and concludes his report with a motion for adoption.

"Mr. Chairman, by direction of the committee, I move adoption of these bylaws."

A second is not necessary as the other members of the committee are seconding the motion.

The chairman then instructs the secretary to read the first article. At this point, the first article may be debated and amended, if necessary. When no other debate is offered, the next article is opened to discussion and amendment and no more discussion is in order on the first article. At the end of the document, when all articles have been presented in this manner, the chairman offers a final opportunity to amend any of the articles.

"Are there further amendments to the bylaws?"

The entire document, as amended, will be adopted in total by a majority vote. Subsequent bylaw amendments will be subject to the amendment process described in the bylaws, including the vote prescribed which is usually at least a 2/3 vote with previous notice.

Chapter 4

Processing a Motion

Too many meetings across this country deteriorate into barely controlled chaos because the members and officers don't know how to process motions properly. Groups often discuss a question without a motion having been made, and when they think they have reached a consensus on the matter, the chair asks for a motion. What follows is a lot of "so-moveds" and "so-be-its" and the assembled members have no idea what they are voting for much less where they are on the agenda! This chapter is designed to bring some understanding to the motions process.

A main motion is the mechanism by which a society introduces business for consideration. A subject is not in order for discussion unless it has been introduced in the manner described in this chapter.

During an actual business meeting, the steps described here will occur so quickly that they are hardly noticed by the unpracticed member, but each step has a purpose and is important to the process.

RISE AND ADDRESS THE CHAIR

In very small groups, a member may remain seated to address the chair. But in groups larger than a committee, members should always stand when speaking. In very large groups there may be microphones provided, in which case members must step to one of the microphones and wait to be recognized.

RECEIVE RECOGNITION

The chair will assign the floor to members in an orderly and timely fashion. A member may speak only when he has been recognized by the chair and has been assigned the floor.

STATE THE MOTION

The correct terminology for introducing a motion, which can be done by any member, is *"I move that..."*

The motion should be in straightforward language so others may easily and rapidly understand it, and it should always be stated in the affirmative.

Motions should include no more than one single item for consideration. This rule differs considerably from a corresponding rule in governmental legislatures where unrelated motions are often attached to a main motion.

In the event of a lengthy motion, the member should write it out and hand it to the president after reading it to the assembly.

The maker of the motion has the right to speak first and last during debate. He may not speak against his motion but, if so persuaded by debate, he may vote against it.

SECOND THE MOTION

The correct terminology for seconding a motion is *"I second the motion,"* or *"Second!"*

This is a crucial aspect of the motion-making process because it indicates that more than one person (the maker of the motion) wishes to spend the time of the assembly on the issue.

The fact that a motion was seconded should be recorded in the minutes. The name of the member who seconded the motion is not of interest and is, therefore, not listed in the minutes.

If the presiding officer does not hear a second, he may ask, *"Is there a second?"* If no second is forthcoming the motion dies for lack of a second. Often a member will second a motion to which he is opposed for the express purpose of having the assembly decide the question once and for all.

One who seconds the motion may speak and vote against it.

CHAIR STATES THE MOTION

When the chair has heard a second he states the motion. *"It has been moved and seconded that we purchase a file cabinet for the secretary's records. Is there discussion?"*

At this point, and not before, the motion becomes the property of the assembly and must be disposed of by the assembly. There are many parliamentary options available for the disposal of motions and we will discuss most of them in this and following chapters.

Motions do not include debate. However, occasionally it is wise to include in the wording of a motion, the rationale behind it. In that case a resolution may be proposed. A *resolution* is a formally drafted motion including a preamble of *Whereas* clauses explaining rationale. It is always written out, with a copy given to the chair.

> *"Whereas, The secretary of this society has been directed to file all records of the society for the past 25 years, and*
>
> *Whereas, The records have been stored in boxes in the basements of various secretaries where they have been damaged or lost, therefore be it*
>
> *Resolved, That the secretary be allocated funds for the purchase of a file cabinet in which to store the society's records, and be it further*
>
> *Resolved, That the secretary be authorized to make such a purchase at his own discretion."*

A resolution does not require a preamble and should never have it included purely for the sake of form. A resolution is totally acceptable with only *Resolved* clauses if rationale is not necessary for the records. In the above example, the resolution involves two parts: 1) authorizing funds and 2) authorizing purchase.

MEMBERS DEBATE THE QUESTION

At this point members may discuss the pending question in free and full discourse, expressing ideas and points of view on the subject. In this way, the general wisdom of the group is encouraged so that the best final solution is achieved.

It is obvious that rules of decorum and debate must be enforced for the purpose of having an orderly and fair discussion. Members may aid in moving the proceedings along in a timely and efficient manner by understanding and adhering to the rules of debate.

The general parliamentary rule is that each member may speak twice for ten minutes each time, but no one may speak the second time until everyone who wishes to do so has spoken once.

Obviously, if the above rule were exercised for each motion and many people wished to speak, little business could be accomplished in the relatively short time that most groups want to spend on business.

Therefore, debate is often limited by a society through its standing rules, convention rules, or by a motion to limit debate. This will be discussed in Chapter 9.

The maker of the motion has the right to be the first and last speaker in debate on the question. He may not speak against his own motion, though he is free to vote against it if he has been so persuaded through the debate process.

Members may not yield unused debate time to other members. This differs from legislative bodies where time is often yielded to other members.

Members must address the chair and never address other members directly. All debate and questions or inquiries must be made through the chair who will in turn direct a response from the appropriate member.

CHAIR PUTS THE QUESTION

When there is no further debate, or the time for debate has ended, the chair "puts the question," a parliamentary term meaning he puts the question to a vote. It is wise, if any discussion has taken place, to restate the motion so that all members have a clear understanding of the wording.

"The pending question is that we purchase a file cabinet for the secretary's records. As many as are in favor of this motion say 'yes' (Pause) **Thank you."**

"As many as are opposed to this motion say 'no' (Pause) **Thank you."**

The chair announces the results in a clear and unmistakable manner.

"The yeses have it, the motion is carried, and the secretary is instructed to purchase a file cabinet for storing our records."

or

"The noes have it, the motion is lost, and a file cabinet may not be purchased."

The chair announces the results in three separate ways so that there can be no misunderstanding by stating 1) which side prevailed, 2) if the motion was carried or lost, and 3) the action resulting from the decision.

Even if the affirmative vote sounds or appears unanimous, the chair is duty bound to ask for the negative vote. In the interest of democracy, this step must not be omitted.

When giving voting instructions, the chair should be as clear as possible in his language. "Those opposed, same sign" is a confusing and archaic custom that should never be used. This is tantamount to asking someone to say "yes" when he means "no," and it causes great confusion among the members.

VOTING METHODS

Voice vote – "Yes (Aye)" and "No (Nay)"

Show of hands – for small groups

Rising vote – to verify the vote

Roll call – checks the attendance as well as vote

Ballot – assures voters' secrecy

General consent – for routine matters
Chair states, *"If there are no objections..."*
Any member can and should object if he feels the need.

Mail or Proxy voting must be authorized in the bylaws

The Secretary to cast one ballot – poor idea and must be authorized in the bylaws

TYPES OF VOTES

Majority – any number greater than half the votes cast

Plurality – the most votes cast regardless of majority

2/3 vote – 2/3 of votes cast

Tie vote – same number for and against – motion lost

Chapter 5

Nominations and Elections

The bylaws usually prescribe the procedure for nominations and elections, but when the rules are silent on these matters, the parliamentary method is as follows.

NOMINATIONS

Most organizations elect a nominating committee whose task it is to seek out candidates for office who are willing, qualified and eager to serve in some capacity. All nominees must consent to having their names placed in nomination. Certainly, no one can be elected to office who is unwilling to serve.

Members of the nominating committee may be nominated for office under the premise that they may not be denied a basic right of membership (to seek and hold office) in order to serve the organization as a committee member.

After the nominating committee has reported, the chair calls for further nominations from the floor. At this time members may nominate candidates for office. There is no second required for nominations, but a second is not out of order if one wishes to indicate endorsement of a candidate. No one may nominate more than one person for an office until everyone else has had a chance to offer nominations for that office.

The motion to close nominations is generally not in order in ordinary deliberative assemblies if any member is seeking the floor in order to make a nomination. The nominations will be closed by the presiding officer when it is obvious that there are no more nominations forthcoming. In the rare event that the motion to close nominations is made, it requires a 2/3 vote, while to reopen nominations requires a majority vote.

ELECTIONS

When the bylaws are silent on the matter of elections, an organization may choose one of two options, depending on its needs.

Nominations and elections can be held for each office in succession. For example, nominations for president may be made and the election for president held before nominations from the floor are open for vice president, and so on. Using this method, a candidate for president who is not elected may be placed in nomination for another office. This works best in small assemblies.

The second method of election is to complete nominations for all offices before an election is held. This works best for large groups and there is usually one single ballot.

This latter method requires tellers to oversee the balloting, to distribute, to collect and count the votes, and to report the outcome of the election in detail to the assembly. The president may appoint tellers to this task or, depending on custom, the nominating or elections committee can handle the tellers' duties.

TELLERS' DUTIES

The tellers must count the ballots and determine that there is one ballot per certified voter. After the election the tellers retire to a separate room to tally the votes.

TELLERS' REPORT

Number of votes cast	67
Number necessary to elect	34
Ms. Miller	37
Mr. Smith	17
Ms. Jones	11
Illegal votes	2

The tellers' report is read in full by one of the tellers. This report is for information only and becomes, verbatim, a part of the minutes. The presiding officer then reads the report again and declares each winner duly elected. If a candidate fails to receive a majority, reballoting must be done for that office. No candidate can be dropped from the list of candidates, regardless of how few votes he received or how lengthy the process. In a heated contest, a dark horse candidate may become a welcome compromise.

Chapter 6

Agenda

An agenda is an order of business which will be customarily followed in each business meeting of a society. An organization may adopt its own version or use the commonly accepted one listed below.

Each of these agenda items will be discussed below in more detail. In this chapter one can see the logical flow of business that is made possible by attention to proper procedure.

AGENDA

Call to Order
Reading and Approval of Minutes
Correspondence
Treasurer's Report
Executive Board and Officers' Reports
Standing Committee Reports
Special Committee Reports
Special Order, if any
General Orders
Unfinished Business
New Business
Program, if any
Announcements
Adjournment

CALL TO ORDER

The chair is in the unique position of influencing the tone of meetings over which he presides. It is, therefore, incumbent upon the chair to be knowledgeable about the rules, evenhanded in enforcing them and impartial and fair in his conduct.

A chairman does not relinquish his rights as a member in order to serve as presiding officer and so is entitled to vote when the vote is by ballot. The chair does not vote when the vote is by voice or show of hands. He may, however, cast a vote to break a tie should it occur in either of these instances. He may also cast a vote to create a tie. In either case he will have the support of only half of the assembly, thus putting him in an unenviable position.

The presiding officer has the duty to know what business is to come before the society at each meeting. The chair constructs the agenda by conferring with the secretary and committee chairmen.

The chair should have in his possession at each meeting the following items:

- a copy of the society's rules (bylaws, standing rules, etc.)
- a copy of the parliamentary authority named in the bylaws
- a list of the committees and their members
- a copy of the agenda

Additionally, it is often helpful to have a symbol of authority such as a gavel, and a time piece.

The chair, after determining a quorum, will call the meeting to order by a light rap of the gavel (optional) and announce *"The meeting will please come to order."* Promptness and punctuality are crucial courtesies to be shown to the assembly by calling a meeting to order exactly on time.

If opening exercises are customary, they would be held immediately after the call to order. There may be an invocation or Pledge of Allegiance to the American flag or a pledge to the ideals of the organization or a combination of these exercises. Protocol demands that items be taken up in the following order: God, country, and family. For example, the invocation would be first, the national pledge second, and the organizational (family) pledge last.

A roll call may be taken at this time, if one is customary.

READING AND APPROVAL OF MINUTES

The chair announces the next item of business by saying, *"We will now hear the reading of the minutes by the secretary."*

The secretary should be ready to read the minutes with no delay. There should be no fumbling with papers or other disruption as the secretary tries to get ready to read the minutes. He should have the official copy at hand, having transcribed them promptly after the previous meeting. This cannot be overstated.

The secretary should always bring the minutes book with the minutes of at least the past year in addition to all pertinent records such as bylaws, committee roster, etc. and a duplicate of the president's agenda.

The agenda, of course, would have been prepared well in advance through the combined efforts of the president and secretary.

MINUTES

There are almost as many forms of minutes as there are secretaries to write them. Some groups enter minutes in a bound book while others keep current minutes in a loose leaf binder and have them professionally bound at the end of each year or every few years. Some groups even use a sewing machine to bind their minutes. Still others publish minutes in organizational magazines and newsletters.

Although there is much latitude in the *form* for minutes, there is much less leeway for the *contents* of minutes. Since the minutes are a written record of what actually happened in a meeting, as opposed to what was said, there are some very specific items that must be recorded. The minutes should always be written in the third person and always in prose rather than sentence fragments or telegraph style.

The first paragraph of any minutes should contain the following:

1. The kind of meeting (regular, special, adjourned, etc.)
2. The name of the assembly
3. The date and time of the meeting
4. The fact that the presiding and recording officers were present or, in their absence, who substituted
5. Whether the minutes of the previous meeting were approved as read or as corrected

The body of the minutes should contain the following:

- All main motions stated in full, with the name of the maker and the fact that it was seconded, and action that was taken (carried or lost). In some societies the name of the maker of the motion is also omitted from the minutes. However, many organizations feel the need to have a record of members' involvement in legislation. In either case, the name of the seconder is not important.

- All points of order or appeals (see Chapter 9), whether sustained or lost.

- The body of the minutes should include a separate paragraph for each subject. Subject titles in the left margin are helpful for future reference, but this is a matter of custom or preference.

- The last paragraph should state the hour of adjournment.

When a committee report is of great importance or should be recorded to show the legislative history of a measure, the assembly can order it "to be entered in the minutes," in which case the secretary copies it in full in the minutes. Otherwise, a committee report is attached to or filed with the minutes.

When a count has been ordered or the vote is by ballot, the number of votes for each side is recorded in the minutes.

The name of a guest speaker and his subject may be recorded, but no effort should be made to summarize his remarks.

The phrase "Respectfully Submitted" before the secretary's signature represents an archaic and outdated contrivance and is no longer considered proper. The secretary's name and title, "Chris Jones, Secretary," and signature are sufficient.

In correcting minutes the secretary simply draws a line through the error, being careful not to obliterate it, and writes the correction in the margin beside the error or, if space permits, directly above the error. For this reason, double spacing as well as wide margins, are helpful but this, too, is a matter of preference or custom.

The office of secretary is, in this author's view, the single most important elected office. The secretary has responsibilities which are crucial to the society: these include updating and maintaining all written records of the organization including bylaws, standing rules, minutes of past and current meetings, committee reports and credentials for delegates.

The secretary shares the responsibility, unless the bylaws state otherwise, of preparing an agenda for the next meeting, indicating specific items of business due for introduction. The secretary, further, has a duty to submit the agenda to the president allowing ample time for that officer to make changes, to confer with committee chairmen, and to prepare for the meeting.

An additional duty of the secretary is to preside, in the absence of the president and vice president, until a chairman pro tem is elected as the first item of business.

After the reading of the minutes the chair asks, *"Are there corrections to the minutes?"* An addition of course, would be a correction, therefore asking for "corrections or additions" is redundant. After a pause to allow members to offer corrections the chair proceeds, *"Hearing none, the minutes are approved as read."*

CORRESPONDENCE

Correspondence may be read at this point in the meeting by the secretary or at other points by committee chairmen or by whomever and whenever it seems most appropriate. Only correspondence pertaining directly to the organization should be read. Junk mail or solicitations beyond the purpose of the society should be discarded by the president and/or secretary.

TREASURER'S REPORT

The treasurer's duties include handling the funds of a society and making regular reports of the financial status as well as any other related duty as specified in the bylaws.

The treasurer's report is not adopted but is filed for audit. Financial records are usually audited annually by a committee of members or by a professional CPA or auditing firm. The auditor's report is adopted by the society.

What follows is the written form of the treasurer's report.

```
Balance on hand, January 31, 1990        $ _____   (1)
    Receipts              $ _____
                          $ _____
                          $ _____
    Total Receipts                                 (2)
    Subtotal                      $ _____
    Disbursements:        $ _____
                          $ _____
                          $ _____
            Total Disbursements                    (3)
    Balance as of February 28, 1990   $ _____   (4)
```

In his oral report, the treasurer will read items 1, 2, 3, and 4. Item 4, the current balance as of the meeting date, is the only figure recorded in the minutes.

The treasurer should be prepared to answer questions concerning specific receipts and disbursements but should not take time to enumerate them unless so ordered by the assembly.

EXECUTIVE BOARD AND OFFICERS' REPORTS

The Executive Board and its membership composition must be established in the bylaws. In the absence of such a provision, a society may not establish an executive board without first amending the bylaws by the prescribed method.

Usually the secretary or president gives the board report, but it may also be given by a vice president or any other board member instructed to act as the reporting officer.

Any other officers wishing to report would be called upon in the order in which they are listed in the bylaws.

STANDING AND SPECIAL COMMITTEE REPORTS

A committee is made up of one or more individuals, usually members, who are elected or appointed to do one or more of the following tasks: 1) consider a matter more fully than is practical in the society's business meetings, 2) investigate or research a matter (such as comparing prices), and 3) take action on behalf of the organization.

Standing committees are established in the bylaws and are called upon for reports in the order in which they are listed. They have a continuing function which they perform throughout the existence of the organization.

When there are both standing committee and special committee reports, the standing committee reports will be heard first.

Special committees are also known as *select* or *ad hoc* committees. They are appointed to perform certain specific tasks, and when the final report of the committee is given indicating the completion of the assigned task, the special committee is automatically dissolved.

A committee report is a statement agreed upon by a majority of the committee and reflects the consensus of the members.

A written committee report is a statement agreed upon by a majority of the committee and reflects the consensus of the members.

It need not be addressed or dated as it will be noted in the minutes which are dated and to which the report will be attached. A written committee report should be in prose and written in the third person. The minutes of the committee meetings are *not* the report. Minutes are the property of the committee and, unless otherwise ordered by the appointing body (the parent organization who created the committee), are not to be available to anyone other than committee members.

A written report may be signed by the chairman alone, in which case he should list his title. It may be signed by the entire committee, in which case the chairman's name is first and his title is not listed. In either case, the words "Respectfully Submitted" are not used as they represent an archaic and outdated style and are no longer appropriate.

In the society's business meetings, the chair should make it his business to know which officers and committees have reports and should refrain from calling on committees that have nothing to report.

A reporting member rises, addresses the chair and begins the report by identifying his committee.

"Mr. President, the Membership Committee reports that..."

or

"Mr. President, the Special Committee on the Founders' Day Picnic reports that..."

If the committee report includes a recommendation for action by the assembly, the report should conclude with an implementing motion.

"Madam President, by direction of the Founders' Day Picnic Committee, I move that we register an entry in the County Historical Display Contest."

This motion does not need a second from the floor because the members of the committee in favor of the motion are, in effect, the seconders.

The chair immediately states the motion as pending business. If the committee report was for information only, the correct procedure is to hear it and thank the reporting member. Written reports are filed with the minutes. Oral reports must be sufficiently brief that the secretary is able to record the entire report verbatim. For obvious reasons, it is generally expected that a report be submitted in writing.

For more information on expediting business in boards and committees see Chapter 7.

SPECIAL ORDERS

Special orders are those items of business which have been postponed to a specific time in a meeting and, by a 2/3 vote, have been given the designation of "special order." These orders must then be taken up at the specified hour even if it means interrupting business in progress, with few exceptions. For example, during debate on an issue, you realize that certain members who could effect the outcome of a vote are absent and, due to prior commitments, could not attend the next meeting before 2:00. Therefore you say, *"I move to postpone this matter to the next meeting and make it a special order for 2:30."* (requires 2/3 vote) As a result, the postponed question must be taken up at 2:30 (and not before) in the next meeting. If you had not specified a time, this special order would be taken up before general orders.

GENERAL ORDERS

General orders are those questions which have been postponed to the next meeting but have not been given the special order designation.

The president must know if there are any special or general orders and is duty bound, under this heading, to announce each one in its proper order for consideration by the assembly.

UNFINISHED BUSINESS

Just as with committee reports, the president should make it his business to know what business was not finished at the previous meeting and announce each item in order. If there is no unfinished business, the heading is not even announced. The president simply goes on to announce new business.

The term "old business" is considered poor form and is no longer used.

NEW BUSINESS

New subject items may be introduced by members at this time. Motions to take from the table (see Chapter 9) may also be made under this heading.

NOTE: An assembly may not be required to decide a question more than once in any given session, except through the process of reconsideration, rescind, or amendment of something previously adopted. Under this heading, then, essentially brand new questions are in order.

PROGRAM

Some organizations customarily have an entertaining or educational program, which often includes a guest speaker but may be offered by members. In any case, this is the point in the agenda when such a program is usually presented. However, it may be taken up, by special rule or by suspending the rules, anytime in the meeting.

ANNOUNCEMENTS

Announcements are in order as the final agenda item before adjournment. Previous notice of intention to offer a motion at the next meeting may be given at this point.

ADJOURNMENT

When there is no further business to be introduced, no announcements to be made, and no member is attempting to obtain the floor, the president may adjourn the meeting by a tap of the gavel and an announcement that the meeting is adjourned.

"There being no further business, (Pause briefly) *this meeting is adjourned."*

For details of the privileged motion to Adjourn, see Chapter 9.

Now that we have seen how an organization makes its own rules and conducts business within their framework, it is time to look at the subordinate groups called boards and committees to see how they function.

Chapter 7

Expediters
for Boards
and Committees

The bulk of the work of an organization is accomplished through the efforts of its boards and committees. It is far too cumbersome for the entire membership to deal with the specifics of many proposals. Committees on the other hand, are especially designed to consider, investigate and sometimes take action on behalf of the larger parent group.

Committees and small boards of a dozen or so members have a special set of rules which allow for a more informal conduct of business. This facilitates the proceedings immensely and allows the maximum work to be accomplished in the minimum time. These special rules of conduct are as follows:

1. Members may remain seated throughout the meeting, even while making motions and debating.

2. A motion cannot die for lack of a second.

3. Members may speak as often and as long as is necessary to give their business full consideration.

4. Members may speak informally without a motion pending.

5. The chairman may remain seated throughout the meeting, even when putting a question to a vote.

6. The chairman may make motions and discuss pending questions the same as any other member.

7. In the case of committees, the chairman is not an administrative officer in the usual sense. She is merely the presiding officer.

8. Motions to reconsider a vote can be made and taken up at any time, no matter when the vote to be reconsidered was taken.

9. A vote may be reconsidered as often as the committee members need in order to complete their task.

10. The motion to reconsider can be made by anyone who did not vote on the side that lost which means anyone who voted on the winning side, or anyone who did not vote, whether through abstention or absenteeism.

11. When a committee or board is considering a matter of great import, it may hold hearings at which time members of the assembly have an opportunity to appear and present their views to the board. However, during the committee or board deliberation on the topic, only members of the committee or board are allowed to be present. The exception to this rule is public boards which are governed by what is commonly known as "sunshine laws" (which are dealt with by open meetings statutes). Law specifics vary from state to state. When one is serving a public constituency, by appointment or election, one is obliged to become conversant with the laws concerning the particular board.

12. If a prescribed portion of the board is elected or appointed at regular intervals, each time new members are named a new board is said to be formed. All unfinished business falls to the ground when the terms expire. Those items may be introduced to the new board as new business and are treated the same as any other new business. Filling a vacancy would not have this effect.

13. The minutes of a board or committee are the property of the board or committee and should never be read to the assembly unless specifically ordered by the assembly.

14. A board or committee may not appoint a subordinate group or authorize action in its behalf unless so ordered by the parent or appointive group.

OTHER COMMITTEE TYPES

When an entire assembly wishes to spend more in-depth time on a question using the less formal constraints offered by rules of conduct for committees, there are three options available, depending on the size of the assembly.

- **Committee of the Whole** is used for groups of more than 100.
- **Quasi** (As If In) **Committee of the Whole** is for groups of 50 to 100.
- **Informal Consideration** is for small groups of less than 50.

Generally speaking, the larger the group the more formality is required to conduct business. These forms are rarely used, but are excellent options under the right circumstances such as when more than two choices must be considered simultaneously. It should be noted that Committee of the Whole differs significantly from its legislative counterpart.

Chapter 8

Classification of Motions

Business is brought before an organization by means of a *main motion* proposing that the group take action. Language for making such a motion is found in Chapter 4.

When a question is introduced and becomes the property of the assembly, members have a wide range of options for disposing of the question. It can be discussed and voted on as it was originally proposed. Or it can have applied to it any number of parliamentary motions designed to aid the assembly in determining the preferences of the majority and in accommodating its members' comfort and convenience.

These parliamentary motions are divided into three classifications; *Privileged Motions, Subsidiary Motions,* and *Incidental Motions.*

Privileged and Subsidiary motions are each assigned a rank. Each takes precedence over motions of lower rank and each yields to motions of higher rank. Each of these motions will be discussed separately in the next chapter.

At this point, before proceeding to the details of each motion, it is important to understand their rank, order, and relationship to each other.

SUBSIDIARY MOTIONS

These motions take precedence over one another in graduating steps from #2 (lowest ranking) to #8 (highest ranking). They are designed to be applied to the main motion (#1 in ranking order) and, when appropriate, to each other.

The motion to *Lay on the Table* is often misused to kill a motion. Its actual purpose is to lay the question aside temporarily in order to handle business of a more pressing nature and then to take the tabled item from the table for consideration as soon as possible.

SUBSIDIARY MOTIONS

Name	Purpose
8. Lay on the Table	To temporarily lay aside a question
7. Previous Question	To end debate
6. Limit or Extend Debate	To change the general debate parameters
5. Postpone to a Set Time	To delay action on a question and control precisely when it will be considered
4. Refer to Committee	To obtain additional information
3. Amend	To modify the question
2. Postpone Indefinitely	To kill the question

It is the highest ranking subsidiary motion and would be in order, for example, while a motion to *Refer to Committee* is being discussed.

When a subsidiary motion is made, it is always made in connection with pending business and the option it offers takes precedence over the business it interrupts. At that point, the subsidiary motion is the pending question and must be decided before the main question or any lower ranking subsidiary motions are processed.

For example, while the assembly is debating the advisability of referring the main question and its amendments to a committee, the motions to *Amend* and to *Postpone Indefinitely* would not be in order. If a member makes one of these motions, the chair should immediately rule the motion out of order by saying, ***"That motion is not in order at this time. The question before us is on referring to committee. Is there further discussion?"***

The chair must *know* the ranking motions and be conversant with their priority. For that reason, it is wise for the chairman to have before him at the podium a motions chart such as the ones found at the beginning of Chapter 9. Using these or similar charts, one can see at a glance which motions are and are not in order at any given time, which can be debated and amended and what kind of vote is required to decide each question.

PRIVILEGED MOTIONS

The privileged motions are the highest ranking classification and they contain a ranking within their class. Details of each motion will be discussed in Chapter 9.

PRIVILEGED MOTIONS	
Name	**Purpose**
13. Fix the Time to Which to Adjourn	To set the time when the meeting will continue
12. Adjourn	To end the meeting
11. Recess	To pause briefly during the meeting
10. Raise a Question of Privilege	To attend to matters of comfort, accuracy, confidentiality, or convenience concerning members or the assembly
9. Call for the Orders of the Day	To compel adherence to the agenda

INCIDENTAL MOTIONS

While these motions have no special rank in relation to themselves or the other motions, their nature of urgency relative to the business at hand requires that most incidental motions be handled before consideration of the pending question can continue.

These are the most frequently used incidental motions. Each must be dealt with immediately when made, provided it is legitimately in order. For example, a point of order must be made immediately upon discovery of a breach of procedure. After the business is completed, even if it contained a breach of conduct, it is too late to call a point of order.

INCIDENTAL MOTIONS

Name	Purpose
Point of Order	To call attention to a breach of procedure
Appeal Decision of Chair	To require the assembly to decide the correctness of the chair's decision
Suspend the Rules	To lay aside a rule temporarily
Object to Consideration	To prevent the assembly from dealing with a particular question
Division of the Question	To prevent two separate questions from being considered in one motion
Division of the Assembly	To compel a standing vote on a question when the result is doubted
Consider Seriatim	To consider paragraph by paragraph
Point of Information	To obtain facts on the substantive issue or the chair's opinion on the parliamentary situation
Object to General Consent	To force a voice vote on a motion
Withdraw a Motion	To prevent one's own motion from being considered

SECOND CHANCE MOTIONS

There are four motions which actually give an assembly a second chance to deal with a question. Grumme calls these motions Restoratory Motions because they do restore the main question to the assembly for action. Robert refers to these by the cumbersome title of Motions that Bring a Question Again Before the Assembly.

Whatever you choose to call them, these motions afford the assembly a second chance to deal with a question. They have no special rank in relation to themselves or other motions.

SECOND CHANCE MOTIONS

Name	Purpose
Take from the Table	To make a tabled question pending again
Rescind or Amend Something Previously Adopted	To undo or modify prior action
Discharge a Committee	To remove a question from a committee's jurisdiction
Reconsider	To bring a question again before the assembly as if there had been no vote

There are special considerations peculiar to each of these motions and they will be discussed in Chapter 9.

In relation to the parliamentary motions there are concepts of precedence, yielding, and adherence to be considered.

Some motions will adhere to the main motion and remain with it as it is temporarily disposed of through a parliamentary measure. For instance, pending amendments (that is, amendments which have been introduced but not finally decided) will adhere to the main motion if it is referred to committee or postponed to the next meeting or laid on the table. But a motion to *Postpone Indefinitely* will not adhere to the main motion if it is referred to a committee.

The adherence quality is mostly a matter of common sense. If it makes sense that a question stick to the main motion, it probably does. If subsequent temporary disposal of the main motion removes the reason for another motion to adhere, it probably does not.

As the chart at the beginning of the next chapter indicates, the motions have specific characteristics peculiar to each one. Anyone interested in correct procedure must be familiar with these characteristics. Some motions require a second, and some do not. Some are amendable and debatable, and some are not. Some motions can be amended with certain limitations, and some may be debated in a limited way. Some require a majority vote or a 2/3 vote, and some are decided by the chair. Some can be reconsidered, and some cannot.

In the final chapter we will take a somewhat detailed look at each motion on the chart. We will discuss its specific characteristics and see exact wording on introducing each motion.

Chapter 9

Motions and Their Functions

This chapter is devoted to the details of the parliamentary motions and their various applications.

On pages 50 and 51 are Charts of Motions which are self-explanatory and can serve as handy tools to check the precedence of motions and the pertinent facts. It is well worth the effort of committing the symbols to memory in order to use this chart effectively in the heat of a meeting. The most seasoned parliamentarian can occasionally get caught up in the proceedings and temporarily need a nudge of the memory.

The chart is highlighted in such a way as to assist the eye in quickly locating needed information.

The remainder of the chapter divides the motions by function and color codes them according to their effect on the proceedings.

WHOA! SLOW DOWN! GO BACK!

Motions found in the *red* section will have a braking effect on the pending business. They will stop the motion, slow it down, or undo it altogether.

FULL SPEED AHEAD! GET GOING!

Motions in the *green* section will expedite business by introducing and modifying motions, and generally will speed up the proceedings.

CAUTION! OOPS! WAIT A MINUTE!

Motions in the *yellow* section pertain to procedural matters effecting pending business.

LET'S ACCOMMODATE

Motions in the *gray* section pertain to the comfort and convenience of the assembly.

When seeking a remedy to a specific problem, one has only to look at the page edges to quickly spot the colored pages. The colors of a traffic light will instantly signal the correct section in which to find a solution: red for *stop*, green for *go*, and yellow for *caution*. Gray is the traditional color for comfort which is where motions may be found which administer comfort and convenience.

CHART OF MOTIONS
── MOTIONS WITH RANK ──

Privileged:

13 Fix Time to Which to Adjourn	S			A	M	R
12 Adjourn	S				M	
11 Recess	S			A	M	
10 Raise a Question of Privilege				Ch		IS
9 Call for the Orders of the Day				Ch		IS

Subsidiary:

8 Lay on the Table	S				M	
7 Previous Question	S				2/3	R*
6 Limit or Extend Debate	S			A	2/3	R
5 Postpone to a Set Time	S	D		A	M	R
4 Refer to Committee	S	D		A	M	R
3 Amend	S	D		A*	M	R
2 Postpone Indefinitely	S	D			M	R(a)

1 Main Motion	S	D		A	M	R

NOTES:

S	=	Second required	R	=	Reconsider
D	=	Debatable	IS	=	Interrupts speaker
A	=	Amendable	IP	=	Interrupts pending business
M	=	Majority vote	(a)	=	In the affirmative
2/3	=	Two-thirds vote	(n)	=	In the negative
Ch	=	Chair decides			

*See explanation on individual motion pages.

CHART OF MOTIONS
MOTIONS WITHOUT RANK

INCIDENTALS:						
Demands						
Point of Order				Ch		IP
Point of Information				Ch		IP
Division of the Assembly				Ch		IP

Objections						
Appeal Decision of Chair	S	D*		M		IP
Object to Consideration				2/3	R(n)	IP
Object to General Consent				M	R(n)	IP

Expediters						
Suspend the Rules	S			2/3		IP
Division of the Question	S		A	M		IP
Consider Seriatim	S		A	M		IP
Withdraw a Motion [by motion S M R (n)]				Ch		IP

Second Chance Motions						
Take from the Table	S			M		
Rescind or Amend Something Previously Adopted	S	D*	A	2/3	R(n)	
Discharge a Committee	S	D*	A	2/3	R(n)	IP
Reconsider	S	D*		M		IP

NOTES:

S	=	Second required	R	=	Reconsider
D	=	Debatable	IS	=	Interrupts speaker
A	=	Amendable	IP	=	Interrupts pending business
M	=	Majority vote	(a)	=	In the affirmative
2/3	=	Two-thirds vote	(n)	=	In the negative
Ch	=	Chair decides			

*These motions are debatable only if the motion to which they are applied is debatable.

"Whoa!
Slow Down!
Go Back!"

MOTION	PAGE						
Lay on the Table	55	S			M		
Postpone to a Set Time	56	S	D	A	M	R	
Refer to Committee	58	S	D	A	M	R	
Postpone Indefinitely	60	S	D		M	R(a)	
Reconsider	62	S	D*		M		IP
Object to Consideration	63				2/3	R(n)	IP
Object to General Consent	63				M	R(n)	IP
Rescind or Amend Something Previously Adopted	64	S	D*	A	2/3	R(n)	
Withdraw a Motion [S M R (n)]	64				Ch		IP

*See exceptions on individual motion pages.

53

LAY ON THE TABLE

From time to time an organization finds the need to *temporarily* set aside a question in order to take up a more pressing matter. The motion to *Lay on the Table* is the mechanism used for this purpose.

It is intended that the question laid on the table will be taken from the table as soon as the pressing matter is resolved. Therefore, after one piece of business has been transacted, an item can be taken from the table.

If a question has not been taken from the table by the end of the next regular session (in an organization meeting at least as often as quarterly), it falls to the ground. It could, however, be introduced as a new motion at a subsequent meeting.

This motion cannot be qualified in any way. A motion to lay a matter on the table until the next meeting is actually a motion to postpone to a set time and should be handled as such.

Lay on the Table cannot be debated, amended, or reconsidered.

Correct wording:
"I move to lay this question on the table."

Motion is seconded.

Chair's response:
"It has been moved and seconded to lay the question on the table. As many as are in favor..."

PERTINENT FACTS

REQUIRES	CAN BE	YIELDS TO	PRECEDES
• Second • Majority Vote		• Privileged Motion • Applicable Incidentals	• All Subsidiary Motions • Pending Incidentals

POSTPONE TO A SET TIME

The purpose of this motion is to delay action on a question within certain time limitations. In assemblies meeting at least as often as quarterly, a question can be postponed until the end of the next regular session.

There are a number of legitimate reasons for an assembly to postpone consideration of a question, such as to hear a scheduled report on the matter or allow opportunity for more members to take part in the consideration.

When a motion is considered on a different day from when it was postponed, individual debate rights begin all over again as if it were a new question.

If the motions to Postpone Indefinitely, Amend, and Commit are pending when the main motion is postponed to a future time, those subsidiaries will adhere to the main motion, that is they will be postponed with the main motion. When the main motion is called up at its proper time, the adhering subsidiaries will likewise become pending again in their order of precedence so that the immediately pending question put to the assembly will be the motion to commit.

Postpone To A Set Time is debatable only as to the advisability of postponing and the time to which it will be postponed.

It is amendable as to the time to which it will be postponed and whether or not to make it a special order.

POSTPONE TO A SET TIME

Correct wording:
> *"Mr. Chairman, I move to postpone this motion to the next meeting."*

Motion is seconded.

Chair's response:
> *"It is moved and seconded that the motion be postponed to the next meeting. Are you ready for the question?"*

At this point, a member could amend by making this motion a special order. The amendment requires a majority vote to carry. If carried, the motion with the special order designation would require a 2/3 vote. Without making the postponed item a special order, a majority vote is required for passage.

PERTINENT FACTS

REQUIRES	CAN BE	YIELDS TO	PRECEDES

• Second
• Majority Vote
	• Debated
	• Amended
	• Reconsidered
		• Limit Debate
		• Previous Question
		• Lay on the Table
		• Privileged Motion
		• Applicable
		  Incidentals
			• Main Motion
			• Postpone
			  Indefinitely
			• Amend
			• Commit
			• Division
			  of Question
			• Consider
			  Seriatim

REFER TO COMMITTEE

This motion is used to send a measure to a committee in order to obtain more in-depth study on the matter.

This motion should include the following details:

- which standing committee, by name, or
- the exact composition of a special committee
- the method of selection of members, and
- instructions to the committee

If "full power" is given, the committee is thereby authorized to act on behalf of the organization in spending or committing funds, entering into a contract, adding to its own membership, and whatever else it deems necessary to complete its assigned task.

If the motion to commit is adopted, the main motion and any pending amendments are sent together to the committee for consideration. When the committee later reports on this motion, the motion and its amendments return in the same condition and wording in which they went to committee.

Debate is limited to the advisability of committing and the details of the committee's composition and instructions. Amendment is similarly limited.

REFER TO COMMITTEE

Correct wording:

> *"I move that the motion be referred to a committee of three to be appointed by the chair to investigate the gym floor options and report at our next meeting."*

or

> *"I move that this motion be referred to the facilities committee with instructions to report at our next meeting."*

Motion is seconded.

Chair's response:

> *"It has been moved and seconded that the question be referred to the facilities committee. Is there discussion?"*

PERTINENT FACTS

REQUIRES	CAN BE	YIELDS TO	PRECEDES

• Second
• Majority Vote
	• Debated
	• Amended
	• Reconsidered
		• Postpone to
		  Set Time
		• Limit Debate
		• Previous Question
		• Lay on the Table
		• All Privileged
		• All Applicable
		  Incidentals
			• Main Motion
			• Postpone
			  Indefinitely
			• Amend
			• Division of
			  Question
			• Consider
			  Seriatim

POSTPONE INDEFINITELY

The purpose of this motion is to kill the main motion without a direct vote.

It is especially useful for sidestepping a badly framed or ill-advised motion whose very consideration might cause repercussions for the organization, such as a motion to endorse a political candidate. While the sole purpose of this motion is to kill the main motion, there are some interesting and useful ramifications of *Postpone Indefinitely*.

For example, debate can include discussion of the main motion. This is the only subsidiary motion that allows debate on the main question as well as the subsidiary and it can, effectively, double one's debating opportunities.

Opponents of the main question use this subsidiary occasionally to test the strength of the main motion. If efforts to kill it fail, they still have a chance to defeat the main motion directly. If passed, this motion suppresses the main question for the remainder of the current session.

If the main question is referred to committee while *Postpone Indefinitely* is pending, this subsidiary motion falls to the ground for the logical reason that the society has decided to consider the matter further rather than kill it altogether.

When debate ends, the chairman puts the question first on *Postpone Indefinitely*. If that motion fails, he announces the main motion as the pending question. If *Postpone Indefinitely* carries, the chair announces the next item on the agenda.

POSTPONE INDEFINITELY

Correct wording:
> *"Madam President, I move to postpone this motion indefinitely."*

Motion is seconded.

Chair's response:
> *"It has been moved and seconded to postpone indefinitely the building of a gymnasium. Is there discussion?"*

After discussion of both the subsidiary motion to Postpone Indefinitely and the main motion, the vote is taken on the subsidiary.

Chair's wording:
> *"The question is on the motion to postpone indefinitely the motion that we build a gymnasium. As many as are in favor of postponing indefinitely, say yes.* (Pause) *Those opposed, say no.* (Pause) *The yeses have it, the motion is carried, and the motion is postponed indefinitely. Is there further business?"*

or

> *"The noes have it, the motion is lost. The question is on the motion to build a gymnasium for our basketball program. Is there discussion?"*

PERTINENT FACTS

REQUIRES	CAN BE	YIELDS TO	PRECEDES
•Second •Majority Vote	•Debated •Reconsidered*	•All Motions	•Main Motion

*Affirmative vote may be reconsidered, but not a negative vote.

RECONSIDER

The purpose of this motion is to bring a question that has been recently decided back to the assembly for new consideration.

There are restrictions as to by whom and when this motion can be made as well as what votes can and cannot be reconsidered. For instance, only a member who voted on the prevailing side, whether for or against the motion, can move to reconsider its vote. This is a protection of the society against an unhappy loser who seeks to disrupt with renewed motions to reconsider.

In organizations meeting as often as quarterly, but having regular sessions of one day or less, the motion must be made on the same day as the vote to be reconsidered was taken. In conventions of several days duration, the motion can be made on the same day or the next day. While some parliamentarians disagree with this rule, it is nonetheless legitimate. When the limitations have expired, the assembly may still reconsider the vote by moving to Rescind or Amend Something Previously Adopted.

It should also be noted that the *making* of this motion has a higher rank (it can interrupt pending business) than its *consideration*, which has only the same rank as the motion whose vote is proposed to be reconsidered. The effect of *making* the motion to *Reconsider* is to suspend action ordered by the motion proposed to be reconsidered. Thus the *making* of the motion has a higher rank than its *consideration*.

Correct wording:
> *"I move to reconsider the vote on building a gymnasium. I voted for the motion."*

Motion is seconded.

Chair's response:
> *"It has been moved and seconded to reconsider the question of building a gymnasium. Is there discussion on reconsidering?"*

OBJECT TO CONSIDERATION

Occasionally a question will come before the assembly which may be beyond the purview of the organization. A member must immediately object to consideration or the opportunity will be lost.

The chair may decide the issue, subject to appeal. The chair also has the option to put the question, in which case a 2/3 vote will prevent consideration of the offending motion.

See Chart of Motions for characteristics.

OBJECT TO GENERAL CONSENT

General consent is an excellent method of voting on routine matters. The chair states, *"If there are no objections* (Pause) *we will..."* This constitutes a bona fide vote and is very useful in moving along the business of the society.

Occasionally, however, a chairman gets carried away with the speed of general consent and begins to use it inappropriately ("If there are no objections to paying the officers' expenses to the national convention in Las Vegas...").

In such cases, a member can and should object to general consent and insist the chair take a formal vote.

Correct wording:
   "I object!"

See Chart of Motions for characteristics.

RESCIND or AMEND SOMETHING PREVIOUSLY ADOPTED

There is no time limit on these motions. Their purpose is to correct hastily adopted motions or to undo unwise or incorrect actions.

A 2/3 vote is required for emergency, on-the-spot adoption or a majority vote if previous notice has been given to all members.

Any action that has been carried out cannot, of course, be rescinded or amended. However, the unexecuted portion of a motion may be rescinded or altered by this means.

Correct wording:

> *"I move to rescind the motion on the gym floor that was adopted at the June meeting."*

See Chart of Motions for characteristics.

WITHDRAW A MOTION

This motion is in the nature of a request and can be made only in the interval between the making of the motion and the chair stating it, without requiring a vote.

After the main motion has been stated by the chair it becomes the property of the assembly and only the assembly can give permission for withdrawal. This permission can be done by general consent or by a majority vote.

When a motion has been withdrawn, it is as if it had never been made. It can be made again at a later date or even at the same meeting.

"Full Speed Ahead! Get Going!"

MOTION	PAGE					
Main Motion	67	S	D	A	M	R
Amend	68	S	D	A*	M	R
Limit (or extend) Debate	70	S		A	2/3	R
Call for the Order of the Day	71				Ch	IS
Previous Question	72	S			2/3	R*
Suspend the Rules	74	S			2/3	IP
Consider Seriatim	74	S		A	M	IP
Take from the Table	75	S			M	
Discharge a Committee	75	S	D*	A	2/3	R(n) IP

*See exceptions on individual motion pages

MAIN MOTION

An original main motion brings business before the assembly. If adopted, it becomes the official act or statement of the organization.

The main motion should be worded in concise, straightforward language in order that its meaning be clearly understood. It should be stated in the affirmative.

The main motion should contain a single proposition, and it must be within the scope of the organization's objectives and rules and must comply with the laws of the land.

The main motion must be a substantially new subject and not simply a rewording of a proposal already considered and disposed of by the assembly.

If the main motion is in the form of a resolution with a preamble, the resolution is debated and amended before the preamble since changes in the Resolved clauses would likely necessitate changes in the corresponding Whereas clauses.

Correct wording:
> *"Mr. Chairman, I move that we build a gymnasium for our basketball program."*

Motion is seconded.

Chair's response:
> *"It has been moved and seconded that we build a gymnasium for our basketball program. Is there discussion?"*

PERTINENT FACTS

REQUIRES	CAN BE	YIELDS TO	PRECEDES
• Second • Majority Vote	• Debated • Amended • Reconsidered	• All Motions	• No Motions

AMEND

Probably the most used of all the subsidiary motions, *Amend* is used to refine a motion with changes in its wording.

There are five ways to amend a motion:

1. To insert words or a paragraph
2. To add words on the end of a sentence; to add a paragraph
3. To strike out words or a paragraph
4. To strike out and insert words in the same place
5. To substitute a paragraph or document for the original

Amendments must be germane to the motion they propose to modify. There are two classes of amendments. A *primary amendment* modifies the main motion. A *secondary amendment* modifies the primary amendment.

When a secondary amendment is adopted or rejected, another is in order. In this methodical way, the assembly can amend a proposal as much as it wishes, bearing in mind that no more than one primary and one secondary amendment may be pending at any one time.

The processing of amendments begins in reverse of the order in which they were made. The secondary amendment is voted on, then the primary amendment (as amended or not) is voted on and finally the main motion (as amended or not) is put to a vote.

PERTINENT FACTS

REQUIRES	CAN BE	YIELDS TO	PRECEDES
• Second • Majority Vote	• Debated • Amended	• Most Incidentals • Subsidiaries of Higher Rank	• Postpone Indefinitely • Main Motion

AMEND

Correct wording:
> *"Madam Chairman, I move to amend the motion by inserting the words 'with a hardwood floor' after 'gymnasium'."*

Motion is seconded.

Chair's response:
> *"It has been moved and seconded to amend by inserting the words 'with a hardwood floor' after 'gymnasium'. Is there discussion?"*

Discussion is in order on the merits of the hardwood floor only. Secondary amendment is also in order.

Correct wording for secondary amendment:
> *"Mr. Chairman, I move to amend the amendment by inserting the words 'professionally striped' before 'hardwood'."*

Motion is seconded.

Chair's response:
> *"It has been moved and seconded to amend by inserting 'professionally striped' before 'hardwood'. Is there discussion?"*

Discussion is confined to the professionally striped concept only. When putting the question, the chairman will take the vote first on the secondary amendment to professionally stripe, then the primary amendment to install a hardwood floor (striped or not, depending on the first vote), and finally on the main motion as amended or not.

LIMIT (or extend) DEBATE

The general rule of debate is that every member is allowed two speeches of ten minutes each. Obviously, there will be times when the assembly opts to alter this rule.

The motion to change the limits of debate requires 2/3 vote because it is limiting members' rights.

Debate may be changed in two ways:
1. By the number and/or length of speeches allowed, or
2. By the total length of time allowed on a certain subject, either by setting a time for debate to end or setting the number of minutes for further debate on the question.

Debate limitations can be imposed on the immediately pending question only or on all pending questions and should be clearly stated in this regard.

This motion may be amended as to the specifics of limitation.

Correct wording:

"Madam Chairman, I move that at 3:00 p.m. we close debate and put the question."

or

"I move debate on this question be limited to no more than another 20 minutes."

or

"I move we limit debate to 1 speech of 3 minutes for each member."

Motion is seconded.

Chair's response:

"It is moved and seconded that debate be limited to another 20 minutes on this question. The question is on limiting debate. As many as are in favor..."

PERTINENT FACTS

REQUIRES	CAN BE	YIELDS TO	PRECEDES
• Second • 2/3 Vote	• Amended • Reconsidered	• Previous Question • Lay on the Table • Privileged Motions • Applicable Incidentals	• All Debatable Motions

CALL FOR THE ORDERS OF THE DAY

Often, the debate of members takes the assembly far afield of the business at hand, and this motion compels a return to the agenda.

This motion can be made by any member and is decided by the chair. No second is required, and this privileged motion is not debatable or amendable.

Call for the Orders of the Day is a valuable tool at the disposal of the assembly.

Correct wording:
"I call for the orders of the day."

Chair's response:
"The orders of the day have been called for, the next question is..."

PERTINENT FACTS

REQUIRES	CAN BE	YIELDS TO	PRECEDES
• Chair Decides		• Privileged Motions • Applicable Incidentals	• All Subsidiary Motions • All Incidentals except Suspend the Rules

PREVIOUS QUESTION

The single most misunderstood motion is this motion to end debate. Because it is widely misunderstood, it is also widely abused.

A disturbingly large number of presiding officers stop debate immediately when they hear a member shout "Question!" This is an uninformed and irresponsible act that treads heavily on a basic right of membership, namely, to debate. For this reason, many parliamentarians are changing the name of this motion to something more descriptive, such as End Debate or Stop Debate.

By whatever name it is called, a 2/3 vote is required to compel the assembly to stop debate and vote on the pending question.

The previous question can be called on all pending questions. If this motion is made with no qualifications, the order to stop debate would effect only the immediately pending question.

The order to stop debate can be reconsidered only before any vote has been taken under the order.

This motion differs significantly from its legislative counterpart.

PREVIOUS QUESTION

Correct wording:
>   *"I move the previous question."*
>
>   or
>
>   *"I move to close debate on all pending questions."*

Motion is seconded.

Chair's response:
>   *"The previous question has been called. As many as are in favor of stopping debate..."*

This motion is often accomplished by unanimous consent. However, if the chair is in doubt he should take a rising vote, bearing in mind that a 2/3 vote is required to stop debate.

If this motion carries, the chair then states the immediately pending question and puts it to a vote with no further debate or amendment.

PERTINENT FACTS

REQUIRES	CAN BE	YIELDS TO	PRECEDES
• Second • 2/3 Vote	• Reconsidered*	• Lay on the Table • Privileged Motions • Applicable Incidentals	• All Debatable Motions • All Amendable Motions • Limit Debate

*Look for exception on facing page.

SUSPEND THE RULES

Occasionally an organization needs to temporarily remove a rule inhibiting a desired action of the assembly. For example members might want to take up something out of its usual order.

It requires a second and a 2/3 vote to suspend the rules, and only those rules not related to the bylaws or the laws of the land can be suspended.

Correct wording:

"I move we suspend the rules on the order of business and hear the guest speaker immediately."

See Chart of Motions for characteristics.

CONSIDER SERIATIM

Consider seriatim means to consider paragraph by paragraph. This is an excellent mechanism for considering a lengthy resolution or a document with sub parts, such as bylaws.

Each part of the document is read, in order, one at a time. Each part is opened for debate and amendment. When one part is perfected, debate and amendment ends on that part, then the next part is opened for debate and amendment. At the end of this process, members may debate or amend any section again. One vote adopts the whole document. Often this method will be suggested by the chair and adopted by general consent. However, two members can force the issue, and a majority vote will carry it.

TAKE FROM THE TABLE

A motion to take from the table is in order after one piece of business has been transacted.

Any member can move to take a question from the table. However, it is not incumbent upon the presiding officer to call to the attention of the assembly that an item is on the table. Taking from the table items previously laid there is the sole responsibility of the members.

When an item is taken from the table, it returns to the assembly in exactly the same condition as when it was laid on the table. All adhering motions remain intact, and the question is put on each in their order of precedence.

If an item is taken from the table on a subsequent day of the session, debating rights begin anew. But if the matter is laid on the table and taken from the table on the same day, those members who have exhausted their debating rights may not speak again on the question.

DISCHARGE A COMMITTEE

This is the means by which an assembly can take a matter out of the hands of a committee. It is in order before the committee reports on the matter.

A negative vote can be reconsidered.

A 2/3 vote is required or a majority vote if previous notice has been given or a majority vote if the committee fails to do its job.

Adoption of this motion returns the referred question to the control of the assembly.

"*Caution!*
Oops!
Wait A Minute!"

MOTION	PAGE						
Point of Order	79					Ch	IP
Point of Information	79					Ch	IP
Appeal	80	S	D*			M	IP
Division of the Question	80	S		A		M	IP
Division of the Assembly	81					Ch	IP

*See explanation on individual motion pages.

POINT OF ORDER

This motion is used to call attention to a violation of the rules and can be made by any member.

The point must be made immediately at the time of the violation. If debate, for example, has begun on a motion that was never seconded, it is too late to call a point of order. The time to have made the point was before or while the chair stated the question.

Correct wording:
"I rise to a point of order."

or

"Point of order!"

Chair's response:
"State your point."

The chair then rules if the point was well taken or not.

POINT OF INFORMATION

This motion is used to obtain facts from the chair or other members the chair may call upon to furnish such information. The chair decides the question or seeks answers from other members.

The related *Parliamentary Inquiry* is used to obtain information on matters related to parliamentary law.

Correct wording:
"I rise to a point of information (parliamentary inquiry)."

APPEAL

Any two members can appeal from the decision of the chair. One member lodges the appeal and the other seconds the appeal.

However, just as with a point of order, an appeal must be made at the time of the chair's decision. If one piece of business has taken place, the opportunity for appeal is lost.

A majority or tie vote sustains the decision of the chair.

Debatability depends on the nature of the appeal. When an appeal is debatable, each member may speak only once except the chair, who may speak twice. In an undebatable appeal, the chair may give brief rationale when putting the question.

Correct wording:
"I appeal from the decision of the chair."

Motion is seconded.

Chair's response:
"The decision of the chair has been appealed. Shall the chair's decision be sustained? As many as are in favor..."

DIVISION OF THE QUESTION

When a motion contains several distinct segments which could each stand alone, the motion to Divide the Question is in order.

It requires a second and majority vote, and it is amendable.

Correct wording:
"I move to divide the question in order to decide separately the matter of building a gymnasium."

Chair's response:
"If there are no objections, the motion will be divided."

DIVISION OF THE ASSEMBLY

When a member doubts the results of a vote as announced by the chair he can call for a division of the assembly. No second is required, so a single member can compel a rising vote.

The chair is compelled to take the rising vote, but is not required to count it. Often, the result will be sufficiently clear to satisfy the assembly. However, if the chair is in doubt, he may choose to recount it. If not, he may be forced to count by a motion to that effect, requiring a majority vote.

Correct wording:
> *"I call for a division."*

> or

> *"Division!"*

Chair's response:
> *"A division is called. As many as are in favor of the main motion please rise.* (Pause) *Thank you. Be seated. As many as are opposed, please rise.* (Pause) *Thank you. Be seated."*

"Let's Accommodate!"

RAISE A QUESTION
OF PRIVILEGE

There are several motions pertaining to the privileges of the assembly and motion pertaining to personal privileges. When a question of privilege is raised, the chair decides if it is well taken, that is, if it is truly of a privileged nature, worth interrupting business.

When such a question is taken up, it is treated as a request.

Correct wording:
"I rise to a question of privilege."

Chair's response:
"Will the member please state the question?"

Member responds:
"The cigar smoke is offensive. Could we please establish a smoking section?"

Chair's response:
"The question is well taken. All smokers will please sit together on the left side of the aisle."

PERTINENT FACTS

REQUIRES	CAN BE	YIELDS TO	PRECEDES
• Chair decides		• Fix the Time to Which to Adjourn • Adjourn • Recess • Applicable Incidentals	• All Subsidiary Motions • All Incidentals • Call for the Orders of the Day

RECESS

The motion to recess interrupts pending business and proposes a brief break in the proceedings.

Recesses may be called for members to caucus, to await the counting of ballots, or for the comfort of members.

If there is no pending business, this motion does not have the privileged characteristic and is treated as a main motion.

Correct wording:
"I move we recess for 15 minutes."

Motion is seconded.

Chair's response:
"It has been moved and seconded to recess for 15 minutes."

The chair may use general consent or may process the motion by putting to a formal vote.

PERTINENT FACTS

REQUIRES	CAN BE	YIELDS TO	PRECEDES
• Second • Majority	• Amended	• Applicable Incidentals • Adjourn • Fix the Time to Which to Adjourn	• All Subsidiary Motions • All Incidentals • Raise a Question of Privilege • Call for the Orders of the Day

ADJOURN

This privileged motion is unqualified and proposes that the meeting end at once.

When a meeting is adjourned while business is pending, that business will be taken up at the next regular meeting (in societies meeting at least as often as quarterly) under unfinished business.

If the adjournment ends the term of any of the officers, any pending business falls to the ground. It may be introduced at a subsequent meeting as new business.

A qualified motion to adjourn is not a privileged motion.

When this motion is made, the chair may, before taking the vote, apprise the assembly of items needing attention, make announcements, allow the motion to Reconsider to be made but not considered, allow notice to be given and Fix the Time to Which to Adjourn.

Correct wording:
"I move that we adjourn."

Motion is seconded.

Chair's response:
"It has been moved and seconded to adjourn. As many as are in favor..."

PERTINENT FACTS

REQUIRES	CAN BE	YIELDS TO	PRECEDES
• Second • Majority		• Fix the Time to Which to Adjourn • Applicable Incidentals	• All Motions except Fix the Time

FIX THE TIME TO WHICH TO ADJOURN

The motion to *Fix the Time to Which to Adjourn* allows an assembly to continue the present session at a different time and place before the next regular meeting.

EXAMPLE: It is quite late in the April meeting at which the bylaws prescribe the annual election. The April meeting may be adjourned to 30 minutes before the May meeting (or any time in between) in order to comply with the bylaws by holding the election. In May, the "adjourned meeting" is called to order, the business of the April meeting is completed, and the meeting is adjourned in time to call to order the May meeting.

This is an infrequently used motion but is valuable when the need arises, such as when a quorum is not available.

Correct wording:

> *"Mr. President, in light of the late hour and the bylaw requirements concerning our election, I move that when we adjourn, we adjourn to meet here at 6:00 p.m. on April 4th."*

Motion is seconded.

Chair's response:

> *"It has been moved and seconded that when we adjourn, we adjourn to meet here at 6:00 p.m. on April 4th. As many as are in favor..."*

PERTINENT FACTS

REQUIRED	CAN BE	YIELDS TO	PRECEDES
• Second • Majority Vote	• Amended as to Time and Place • Reconsidered	• Applicable Incidentals*	• All Motions

* ie: Point of Order

The End &
The Beginning

A knowledge and understanding of parliamentary procedure is an ongoing, cumulative, lifelong pursuit. This book provides the basis for such a pursuit by offering basic facts, wording and motions.

Goers' Guide is unique in that it eliminates having to deal with the total of a sometimes overwhelming subject.

It should be understood, however, that there is much more to the subject of parliamentary law than is presented in this text. The serious student will use *Goers' Guide* as a springboard from which to launch a comprehensive study.

What follows this chapter is an index for quick reference and a glossary of parliamentary terms. It is often helpful to keep a running glossary to which new terms, as they are encountered, can be added.

For those of you looking for power, you have it in your hand. By understanding the rules of procedure you can more effectively accomplish your goals. Of course, we've all seen people manipulated by one or two with a little knowledge, but the remedy for such abuse is that same knowledge.

It is beautiful and exciting to witness a meeting where the members are well versed in proper procedure. It is equally exciting to seek a remedy among the rules and to discover that there is a rule that speaks specifically to the problem. Or better yet, to find several remedy options from which to choose!

Parliamentary procedure has always been a thrilling subject to this author. It never fails that when I am looking up a particular point, I rediscover another point or two and find myself happily sidetracked.

My wish for you, dear reader, is that you derive a similar joy from this text. Thus my gift to you, THE RULES.

GLOSSARY

Abstain – to refrain from voting.

Adjourn – to terminate a meeting or a session.

Adjourn sine die – "adjourn without day"; used in conventions and legislatures to end the session.

Agenda – an order of business to be followed in a meeting.

Amend – to change a motion.

Appeal – a motion which questions or challenges the chair's decision.

Ballot – a method of voting on paper or by machine keeping the voter's choice a secret.

Board – a subordinate body of an assembly.

Bylaws – the basic rules of an organization.

Chair – the person presiding over a meeting; also refers to the physical station in the meeting hall from which the person presides.

Committee – one or more persons elected or appointed to consider, investigate, and/or take action on certain matters or subjects.

Committee of the Whole – a committee comprised of the entire assembly at a meeting.

Consent – agree to a proposal.

Debate – discussion in a deliberative body on the merits of a pending question.

Decorum – practices and customs for procedure which promote the smooth and orderly conduct of business.

Division of the Assembly – a motion calling for a recount of the vote to verify the announced results. This is accomplished by a standing or rising vote.

Division of the Question – a motion calling for the currently pending motion to be divided into two or more separate questions.

Ex officio – by virtue of the office.

Floor – a speaker is said to have the floor, which is assigned by the chair.

Gavel – usually a wooden mallet, it is the symbol of the chair's authority.

General consent – a method of voting on routine matters, whereby members agree to an action by not raising an objection.

Germane – pertinent to the pending subject, as in the case of a secondary amendment being germane (pertinent) to the primary amendment.

Hearings – times in the meeting of a board or committee when members of the organization can appear and give testimony or opinions on the work of the committee or board.

Incidental Motions – motions relating to or arising out of pending business.

Informal Consideration – a type of committee comprised of the entire assembly whereby the assembly can consider a matter less formally.

Main Motion – a formal proposal by a member in a meeting, that the assembly take certain action.

Majority vote – more than half of the votes cast.

Meeting – the event of an assembly gathering to transact business. Also can be one part of a session.

Minutes – the official written record of the proceedings in a meeting.

Order of business – any established sequence in which it may be prescribed that business shall be taken up at a session; agenda.

Order of the day – an item of business that is prescheduled to be taken up during a given session, day, or meeting, or at a given hour.

Pending business – items of business that have been properly introduced and have not yet been resolved.

Plurality – the largest number of votes to be given any candidate or proposition when three or more choices are possible.

Preamble – one or more clauses beginning with "Whereas" which explain the reasons for a resolution.

Previous notice – announcement of a motion which will be made at the next meeting, including the contents of the motion.

Privileged motions – the five highest ranking parliamentary motions. They interrupt business and they deal with the comfort and convenience of the members.

Pro tem – temporary.

Putting the question – putting the motion to a vote.

Quasi Committee of the Whole – a special committee type which mimics Committee of the Whole in some aspects but is simpler and suited to groups of 50 to 100 members.

Quorum – the minimum number of members who must be present at meetings for business to be legally transacted.

Recess – a short intermission within a meeting.

Regular meeting – the periodic business meeting of a permanent organization held at regular, prescribed times; also known as "stated meeting".

Resolution – a formally phrased motion containing one or more clauses each beginning with "Resolved". Resolutions may, but are not bound to, contain explanatory "Whereas" clauses called a preamble.

Rising vote – a method of voting requiring members to stand as an expression of their vote.

Roll call – a method of voting that also verifies attendance and records how each member votes.

Second – an important step in getting a main motion before the assembly, it indicates to the chair that more than one person is interested in discussing the subject.

Seriatim consideration – paragraph by paragraph.

Session – a meeting or series of meetings devoted to a single agenda.

Special committee – a committee, sometimes called "ad hoc", named to undertake a specific task for a specific time.

Special meeting – a separate session held at a different time from the regular meeting for the purpose of considering one or more items of business listed in the call of the meeting; also known as "a called meeting".

Special orders – postponed items of business guaranteed to be brought up at a certain time; a 2/3 vote is required to create a special order.

Standing committee – named in the bylaws to deal with a particular segment of the organization's business; the terms of members of standing committees coincides with the terms of officers.

Standing rules – rules having to do with the day to day administration of the organization and which are likely to need changing from time to time.

Sustain – uphold.

Tellers – members appointed by the chair to distribute, collect, tally and oversee a ballot vote.

Tie vote – an equal number for each side; motion lost.

Treasurer's report – a financial statement made by the treasurer to the assembly explaining the current financial status of the organization.

Two-thirds vote – 2/3 of those members present and voting.

Unfinished business – any items of business that were not finished at the last meeting; NEVER called "old business".

INDEX